C000149751

DA VI....
A broken code

O f all the women in the Bible, it is Mary Magdalene who has stolen the media headlines in recent years. In 2003 a book reached No. 1 on the *New York Times* best-seller list, and it stayed there for thirty-five weeks. The book was *The Da Vinci Code*, and its author is Dan Brown. On 3 November 2003 fifteen million Americans heard his testimony on the breakfast programme 'Good Morning America', in which he claimed that his book was not just a novel, but scholarly fact—real history. The book soon became a best-seller in the UK where, by the end of 2005, it was running at around 50,000 copies a week. Some forty million copies have been distributed worldwide in over forty languages. A blockbuster movie by Columbia Pictures will be released to seventy-two countries in May 2006. *Time* magazine early in 2005 commented, 'Perhaps it is worth noting that one of the very few books to sell more copies than *The Da Vinci Code* in the past two years is the Bible.'

There must be something more to this novel than a good story, because around ten books have been published challenging its claims—and that figure is rising.

But why should a novel arouse such opposition?

The best way to begin an answer is to take a fast tour of the book—but in case you have not yet read it, don't worry, I will not spoil the story for you. The plot is simple:

On one side of the conspiracy is the Priory of Sion, a secret society dating back to the time of the Knights Templar in the Crusades of the Middle Ages, whose mission is to preserve, at all costs, the true secret of the Holy Grail. When this secret is revealed to the world, which the Priory of Sion is pledged to do at some time, it will correct the false story about Jesus that Christians have been conned into believing over the past seventeen hundred years, and at the same time utterly discredit the Christian church.

On the other side of the conspiracy are agents of Opus Dei, a Catholic society determined to find the Grail and destroy it. Knowing full well the devastating effects should its contents become universally known, they will stop at nothing to eliminate all who stand in their way.

Caught in-between the Priory of Sion and Opus Dei are Robert Langdon, a Harvard professor of iconography and religious art, Sophie Neveu, an agent from the Department of Cryptology of the French Judicial Police, and an eccentric British historian, Sir Leigh Teabing.

The battle is to possess the Keystone which, when its code is broken, will reveal the location of the Holy Grail.

But who is the mysterious Teacher manipulating the hideous orgy of death? And where does the ancient Rosslyn Chapel, seven miles south of Edinburgh, fit the search for the Holy Grail? And what is its connection with La Pyramide Inversée in the Louvre in Paris? And precisely who is that French agent Sophie?

That will do for the story!

The *Da Vinci Code* is an OK novel, but it is not a great read and some find it in places quite tedious. If you are into secret societies, symbols, ciphers, cryptexts, anagrams, cryptograms and the rest, then you may enjoy cracking the codes with the characters. However, if it were not for the undermining of the New Testament Gospels, this book would never have made it to the top. When books discredit Christ, they pay well.

1. Why the fuss?

You may be wondering what all the fuss is about, since not too many of us are bothered one way or the other about the legend of the Holy Grail. Why don't we leave the novelist and his readers to enjoy themselves? If we ignore them, they will eventually go away. Unfortunately, it is not quite as straightforward as that. Whilst the book is undoubtedly a novel and all the characters are fictitious, Dan Brown claims that 'The artwork, architecture, documents, and secret rituals depicted in this novel all exist' and that 'These real elements are interpreted and debated by fictional characters.'

Generously the author concedes, 'While it is my belief that some of the theories discussed by these characters may have merit, each individual reader must explore these characters' viewpoints and come to his or her own interpretations. My hope in writing this novel was that the story would serve as a catalyst and a springboard for people to discuss the important topics of faith, religion, and history.' Dan Brown concludes that, 'The vast majority of devout Christians understand this fact and consider *The Da Vinci Code* an entertaining story that promotes spiritual discussion and debate.'

At first glance this all looks very reasonable; the problem is, in the book there are plenty of 'theories' but no 'discussion' at all. The theories of Randall and Teabing are presented as facts that every intelligent person should know, and claims are made for real documents with no attempt to present another point of view. Sophie is hopelessly outclassed in the debate and quickly concedes all her defences. Whilst interpreting the theories 'is left to the reader', the reader is offered no other side of the debate on which to judge the merits of the arguments. No one, anywhere in the novel, takes an opposite view to that presented by the two academics as fact.

Subtly, Teabing, the eccentric British historian in the novel, when meekly challenged by Sophie on some of his conclusions, suggests mildly that, 'The vast majority of educated Christians know the history of their faith'—the implication being that if you did not realise that all this is fact, then you are out of touch and ignorant. Scattered liberally through the novel are such assertions as 'all academics', 'many scholars claim', 'the vast majority of educated Christians know', with virtually no evidence to back up these wild statements.

The unwary reader may assume that what is claimed in the novel for the 'documents, rituals, organization, artwork, and architecture' is fact. Few readers will trouble to enquire into the evidence, and many will accept the baseless theories of the novel as good reason to remain disconnected from the Bible; they always thought it was nonsense, and now they have strong proof for believing this—proof based on real documents.

How can the reader distinguish between wild imagination and serious academic discussion in a book like this? For example, the claim that the Nag Hammadi Library informs us that Jesus and Mary Magdalene were married is impossible to refute unless readers take the trouble to read the documents for themselves.

A word of advice therefore: Readers would be wise to assume that *all* the conclusions in the novel relating to the Bible are false—until they have had time to check them out.

2. What is the central message of *The Da Vinci Code*?

We cannot attribute any of the 'facts' in the novel as necessarily being the personal beliefs of Dan Brown. He has, as we have seen, carefully tried to distance himself from this charge—though later I will suggest his agenda—so I will refer to them as the views of the novel or of Teabing (the eccentric historian).

1. THE HOLY GRAIL IS MARY MAGDALENE

Tradition has it that the Grail was the cup used by Christ at the Last Supper with his disciples and in which Joseph of Arimathea gathered some of the blood of Christ. However, that is not what the Holy Grail (*San Greal*) is at all. The Holy Grail is none other than Mary Magdalene to whom Jesus was married. The novel maintains that this is 'a matter of historical record'. Jesus had a child from Mary called Sarah. After the crucifixion Mary fled with her child, eventually to France, where the blood line of Jesus intermarried with the French royal family to establish the royal Merovingian line. Thus the words *San Greal* should be divided, and originally were, at a different point, to read *Sang Réal*, Royal Blood. Somewhere in Europe that blood-line—the bloodline of Jesus himself—continues. Somewhere also, the body of Mary is buried and with her, vital documents that will reveal the true story of Jesus and Mary Magdalene.

2. HAIL MARY!

Thus the quest for the Holy Grail is literally 'the quest to kneel before the bones of Mary Magdalene. A journey to pray at the feet of the outcast one, the lost sacred feminine.' She is the 'wronged Queen, entombed with proof of her family's rightful claim to power.'

3. AWAY WITH THE GOSPELS—MATHEW, MARK, LUKE AND JOHN

The earliest Christian documents were not the four Gospels (Matthew, Mark, Luke and John—the word 'Gospel' means 'good news') but the writings of a movement known as the Gnostics. These state quite clearly that Jesus was just a man and not God, that he married Mary Magdalene by whom he had a child, and that he did not die on the cross. More than this, the Gnostics provide the true account that women were the first leaders in the church, and Mary Magdalene was chief among the apostles.

4. ALL CHANGE IN THE FOURTH CENTURY

But then, in the fourth century all was changed. The church wanted to downgrade women and upgrade Christ, so they rewrote the story, which is the four Gospels in the New Testament. These Gospels claim that Jesus is God, he died and rose again, and men are the leaders. All the Gnostic books were hunted down and destroyed. This scheme was masterminded by the Roman emperor Constantine who, for political reasons, embraced Christianity—the new religion was growing so he decided to back the winner. This is how *The Da Vinci Code* explains it: 'Constantine commissioned and financed a new Bible which omitted those gospels that spoke of human traits and embellished those gospels that made him [Jesus] godlike. The early gospels were outlawed, gathered up and burned.'

5. ENTER THE GNOSTIC DOCUMENTS

Until 1945 we possessed virtually none of the Gnostic writings, and all we knew about their beliefs was what the early church leaders wrote when they were attacking the Gnostics. Then, in that year, a collection of Gnostic books was discovered at Nag Hammadi on the banks of the Nile in Egypt. Now we know exactly what they believed. These books, we are told, contain the authentic story about Christ. They reveal what the church for the first three hundred years really believed.

In brief: Jesus was a great man but not God. He married Mary Magdalene and had a daughter by her. The real story of Jesus is in the Gnostic writings, and the four Gospels were imposed on the church around the year AD 325. Everything we have been taught about Jesus since that date is a monumental fraud.

Perhaps you can already begin to see the significance of this 'historical novel'. But is this all true or false? You may or may not want it to be true, depending on your starting point, but the real issue is: how much of this, if any, is historical fact? Also, where does Leonardo da Vinci enter the conspiracy?

3. A glance at the Gnostic Gospels

In December 1945 an Arab peasant, digging for some good soil along the banks of the Nile in Egypt, stumbled across a large earthenware jar containing thirteen papyrus books made up of fifty-two texts. Probably hidden towards the end of the fourth century, these books contain almost all that we have of the writings of the Gnostics themselves. However, they do at least confirm that what the early church leaders wrote about them was accurate.

It is not easy to summarise the beliefs of the Gnostics because they often held widely different views from one another. Writing towards the end of the second century, Irenaeus, the leader at Lyons, complained about the Gnostics: 'Every one of them generates something new, day by day, according to his ability; for no one is deemed perfect who does not develop … some mighty fiction.'

The literature of the Nag Hammadi Library is made up of some of that 'mighty fiction'.

In brief, the Gnostics were not interested in Christian doctrine; they preferred to express their religion in obscure statements and visionary insights which few could understand. The word 'Gnostic' comes from the Greek word for 'knowledge' and it refers to the secret mysteries that they claimed were not available to all. They believed in two gods: the incorruptible God revealed in the New Testament, and the demiurge—an evil god revealed through the Old Testament. Jesus was not God, and anyway he was substituted on the cross by an ordinary man. Salvation is not by Jesus Christ taking our sin and its punishment on the cross in our place, but by grasping a knowledge of the mysteries, receiving the secrets. Salvation is therefore obtained by us from within ourselves.

Let's take a quick look at three of the most significant books in the Nag Hammadi Library.

The Gospel of Thomas is perhaps the most important of the Nag Hammadi documents. It contains nothing of the story of Christ's life, but only one hundred and fourteen sayings allegedly of Jesus. It begins: 'These are the secret sayings which the living Jesus spoke and which Didymus Judas Thomas wrote down.' That is supposedly the apostle Thomas—the one who doubted the resurrection. Apparently Jesus took Thomas to one side and told him secret things. Parts of the Gospel of Thomas bear similarities with the teaching of Jesus. Some are even straightforward quotations which reveal a clear knowledge of the four Gospels, as for example: 'Jesus said, "If a blind man leads a blind man, they will both fall into a pit."' (34), which is clearly taken from Matthew 15:14. But much of it wanders away from the real sayings of Jesus in the four Gospels.

It is interesting to note how the Gospel of Thomas refers to women—remember, this Nag Hammadi Library is supposed to reinstate women as leaders. Here is the very last saying, number 114: 'Jesus said, "I myself shall lead her [Mary] in order to make her male, so that she too may become a living spirit resembling you males. For every woman who will make herself male will enter the kingdom of heaven."'

Perhaps Dan Brown missed this.

Apart from the fact that it was rejected by the early churches, there is one other good reason why we should not take this false gospel seriously: It claims to come from the apostle Thomas, but there is not one scholar who seriously believes that Thomas really wrote it. Why should we trust a writer who pretends to be someone he is not?

The Gospel of Philip does not claim to be the teaching of Jesus, but is a handbook of Gnostic thinking. Much of it is mysterious, and some would like to think 'deep'. Whatever one's view of the Gospel of Philip it is impossible to read it without appreciating by contrast the simplicity and clarity of the four Gospels. Here is a sample of the obscure:

> Light and Darkness, life and death, right and left, are brothers of one another. They are inseparable. Because of this neither are the good good, nor evil evil, nor is life life, nor death death. For this reason each one will dissolve into its earliest origin. But those who are exalted above the world are indissoluble, eternal.

Some of the expressions are heretical, for which the early church leaders rightly condemned it. As an example, here is another passage from the Gospel of Philip in which the Gnostic denial of the Virgin Birth is clear:

> Some said, 'Mary [was] conceived by the Holy Spirit.' They are in error. They do not know what they are saying. When did a woman ever conceive by a woman? … And the Lord would not have said, 'My Heavenly Father' unless he had had another father, but he would have said simply 'My father'.

According to this document, the world came about through a mistake:

> For he who created it wanted to create it imperishable and immortal. He fell short of attaining his desire. For the world never was imperishable, nor, for that matter, was he who made the world. For things are not imperishable, but sons are. Nothing will be able to receive imperishability if it does not first become a son. But he who has not the ability to receive, how much more will he be unable to give?

It is hardly surprising that the early church leaders condemned this kind of teaching. It stood far outside the mainstream of Christian belief.

The Gospel of Mary is supposedly the Mary Magdalene of the Bible. Much of the document has been lost or damaged and it is hardly possible to assess what Mary really said because large sections are missing. As with the previous two books, it is misleading to refer to it as a 'gospel', since we learn nothing about the life and ministry of Jesus. What we have here is mystic teaching attributed to Mary Magdalene. Following the ascension of Christ, the disciples were in despair and it is Mary who rouses them to action and courage. Let the text speak for itself—this conversation apparently took place after Jesus had left the disciples:

> Then Mary stood up, greeted them all, and said to her brethren, 'Do not weep and do not grieve nor be irresolute, for His grace will be entirely with you and will protect you. But rather, let us praise His greatness, for He has prepared us and made us into Men.' When Mary said this, she turned their

hearts to the Good, and they began to discuss the words of the Saviour. Peter said to Mary, 'Sister we know that the Saviour loved you more than the rest of woman. Tell us the words of the Saviour which you remember, which you know, but we do not, nor have we heard them.' Mary answered and said, 'What is hidden from you I will proclaim to you.'

Mary now delivered the secret things that she had learned from Jesus. At the end, Andrew and Peter refused to believe her until Matthew Levi put them to shame— and they all went off to preach the good news. Little more is said about her relationship with Jesus than is recorded above. This book sees Mary Magdalene as a favourite of Jesus and one who possessed a knowledge and spirituality superior to that of the apostles. One commentator, a woman it should be noted, goes so far as to suggest that 'Mary Magdelene's spirituality, which here seems more consistent with the teachings of Christ, is unheard of today.' This is an extremely odd conclusion to most who have read this fragmentary 'gospel'. It does not advance our understanding much apart from confirming the mysteries of Gnosticism.

How can we sum up the Gnostic writings that were lost under the Egyptian sand for so long?

They are not written by those whose names are attached—with this all scholars agree.

They record no history, so we cannot check them out.

They are full of strange and obscure sayings.

Their doctrine is clearly out of line with what the early church leaders were teaching during the first three hundred years.

As one scholar has suitably expressed it: 'Only the rubbish of the second century was destroyed. It is still rubbish.'

4. What about Mary Magdalene in the Bible?

Her story is told in the four Gospels. Mary is not to be confused with the woman referred to in Luke 7 who gate-crashed a party and poured a valuable perfume over Jesus, wiping his feet with her hair; that woman was clearly a converted prostitute and there is no evidence that this was the line of business of Mary Magdalene. It was Pope Gregory who first confused the two in a devotional sermon he gave in AD 591.

However, the four Gospels tell us that Mary Magdalene had been terribly afflicted by evil spirits. She was freed by Christ and joined with a number of other women who took it upon themselves to support Jesus and the disciples out of their own means (Luke 8:2–3). We next find Mary at the cross (Matthew 27:56) and from there she, along with some of the other women, followed the burial party to the private garden of Joseph of Arimathea and identified the exact location of the tomb (Matthew 27:61). When the Sabbath day was over, Mary went to the market with two friends to buy more spices to anoint the body of Jesus (Mark 16:1). In his Gospel, the apostle John focuses upon Mary's lone encounter with Jesus in the garden on the morning of the resurrection (John 20:1–18). Mary was privileged to be the first to see Jesus alive and the first to proclaim his resurrection to the disciples.

This is all that is said about her in the Bible.

• If the church in the fourth century was so intent on writing women out of the picture, as the novel claims, it made a serious blunder in leaving these stories in: Mary Magdalene was the first to witness and announce the resurrection, and she and the other women showed a great deal more courage than the men at the time of the crucifixion of Jesus.

• In addition, there is a great deal more said about Mary Magdalene in the four Gospels than about most of the twelve apostles of Jesus.

• It is also remarkably strange that at the very time the church supposedly wanted to rid the records of the importance of women—sometime in the fourth century—the cult of the veneration of Mary the mother of Jesus should be first appearing.

5. Was Jesus married to Mary Magdalene?

From all that is written about the Nag Hammadi library, a reader might expect that these books are full of evidence to support the marriage between Mary Magdalene and Jesus. Teabing claims that there are 'countless references to Jesus and Magdalene's union.'

In fact, in the Gnostic books there is not one single statement that Jesus and Mary were married.

So, where did the idea come from?

Remember, the theme of *The Da Vinci Code* is that the fourth century church wanted to downgrade women, upgrade men and insist upon celibacy for the priests, so they rewrote the Gospels that we now have. The novel must now ransack the Gnostic documents to find something—anything will do, however tenuous. And there are just two passages.

In the Gospel of Philip that we referred to above, we find one text. But it must be understood that the document is badly damaged and there are parts that are missing, so the dots in brackets mean that part is lost. The novel, in quoting this passage, does not indicate the gaps but simply adds its own words! In the original translation the relevant part reads:

> And the companion of the [...] Mary Magdalene. [...] loved her more than all the disciples, and used to kiss her often on [...]. The rest of the disciples [...]. They said to him 'Why do you love her more than all of us?' The Saviour answered and said to them, 'Why do I not love you like her? When a blind man and one who sees are both together in darkness, they are no different from one another. When the light comes, then he who sees will see the light, and he who is blind will remain in darkness' (The Gospel of Philip 63:34).

The novel adopts the words 'the mouth' in the third blank space, to make it read: 'used to kiss her often on the mouth.' Then Teabing claims that this proves that Jesus and Mary were married—though most readers would doubt that even this constitutes 'proof'!

However, the words 'cheek', 'forehead', or even 'hand' would fit the blank space just as easily. Actually the common first century kiss of fellowship for both male and female was on the cheek, therefore unless we have a strong reason for not doing so, we should insert the word 'cheek'.

So, on the basis of a single document that was never accepted by the early church, was lost under the sand for seventeen hundred years, and when found was damaged beyond repair at the only reference that Jesus kissed Mary Magdalene on the—we don't know where—we are to presume that they were married.

Is that scholarship?

Is it honest?

Remember, this is what the novel calls 'a matter of historical record.'

Imagine what Bible critics would say if Christians used that same kind of evidence to try to prove something!

Isn't it strange how some will doubt the clear and well attested evidence of the four Gospels, and yet are prepared to accept as fact, flimsy evidence read into a small and incomplete section of a torn document that was rejected seventeen hundred years ago?

But there is one other passage. It comes in the Gospel of Mary, where Peter is complaining that Jesus revealed things to Mary that he did not reveal to the other apostles. Levi rebukes Peter with the words:

> If the Saviour made her worthy, who are you indeed to reject her? Surely the Saviour knows her very well. That is why he loved her more than us.

That is all. Surely, if they *were* married this was the very place to say so. Even assuming that this 'gospel' is genuine, is that phrase convincing evidence that Jesus and Mary were husband and wife?

There is no other passage that can be appealed to in any ancient writing with clearer 'evidence' than these two, to support the idea that Jesus married Mary Magdalene—or anyone else. In spite of the wild claims, this is the nearest the Nag Hammadi Library ever gets to suggesting that Jesus and Mary were married.

Yet the novel claims that there are 'countless references to Jesus and Magdalene's union.'

Prof. Darrell Brock, writing on this subject, referred to his own library of the writings of the early church documents: he has thirty-eight volumes 'each of several hundred pages, double columns, in small print', and amongst all this, these are the only two texts that can be appealed to for this theory.

Some evidence!

One New Testament scholar, John Dominic Crossan—who is not known for his support of the reliability of Bible history—humorously responded to the question of whether or not Jesus was married, in this way:

> There is an ancient and venerable principle of biblical exegesis [understanding the Bible] which states that if it looks like a duck, walks like a duck, and quacks like a duck, it must be a camel in disguise. So, let's apply

that to whether or not Jesus was married. There is no evidence that Jesus was married (looks like a duck), multiple indications that he was not (walks like a duck), and no early texts suggesting wife or children (quacks like a duck) … so he must be an incognito bridegroom (camel in disguise).

So, not even the dusty Egyptian library of Gnostic books claims that Jesus and Mary were married.

6. Would it matter if Jesus was married?
In the novel, Teabing suggests that Jesus must have been married because as a Jewish rabbi this was the norm. How do we answer this?

Jesus never claimed to be a rabbi and besides, no one can read his story very far without realising that Jesus hardly fitted the 'norm' of rabbinical life-styles! But, in fact, in the first century, it was not necessary for rabbis to be married, and the strict Jewish community of Essenes was committed to celibacy.

The novel also makes play on the fact that the church in the fourth century needed to make Jesus unmarried so that they could support the growing rule that all priests in the church should be celibate.

If this is the case, the church apparently made another monumental blunder by allowing the story of Peter's mother-in-law to remain in the Gospels (Matthew 8:14)—since Peter is supposed to have been the first pope!

In some ways it would not matter in the least if Jesus had been married. Marriage is pure according to the Bible (Hebrews 13:4) and he would have been the perfect example of the perfect husband. However, the New Testament speaks of the church as the Bride of Christ that will one day be united with her Bridegroom at the marriage supper (Revelation 19:7,9; 21:2,9; 22:17). This is a picture of all Christians finally joining Christ in heaven; this would hardly have made sense to the early church if he already had a wife.

On the other hand, the simple fact is that there is no evidence at all that Jesus was married, and all the evidence points to the opposite. One writer on this subject has pointed out that one of the few things about Jesus that all scholars agree on, even the most critical, is that Jesus was single. That must count for something.

7. How accurate are the 'facts' of the novel?

Most of the media examination of *The Da Vinci Code* focuses on the conspiracy theories involving the supposed Priory of Sion—and it has been consistently discredited on this ground. But this misses the point entirely. Whether or not the Priory of Sion exists as a secret society with a world-shattering secret is not really the question; the crucial issue is what the novel says about the reliability of the Bible. If the Bible is accurate, then even if a Priory of Sion is discovered and its 'secret' of a marriage between Jesus and Mary is revealed, it is the 'secret' that is a fraud, not the Bible.

In other words, if the Bible is true then the conspiracy theory falls.

David Shugarts, a journalist who investigated this novel, claims to have discovered nearly seventy errors of fact, of which over sixty are significant. Here are just a few.

CLAIM NO. 1

In that passage from the Gospel of Philip quoted above, the novel pretends that the word 'companion' means 'spouse'. Teabing claims: 'As any Aramaic scholar will tell you, the word companion, in those days, literally meant spouse.' Not many readers can check this one out.

THE FACTS: The Nag Hammadi Gospel of Philip was written in Coptic, not Aramaic, but at this point the word used is borrowed from a familiar Greek word *koinonos* which means 'associate', 'partner' or 'companion'. The word for a spouse or wife is a completely different word. To claim that *koinonos* meant spouse is a display of either ignorance or dishonesty.

CLAIM NO. 2

The claim of Dan Brown's novel is that our present four Gospels were not compiled until some time in the fourth century; the whole Bible 'evolved through countless translations, additions and revisions. History has never had a definitive version of the book.'

THE FACTS: In all the history of how the Bible came to us, there is no evidence of it *evolving* 'through countless translations, additions and revisions.' The English Old Testament is translated from Hebrew and the New Testament from Greek—that is just one translation for each. There is no evidence that any of the Bible books circulated incomplete before their present form ('additions'), and there is no evidence that any Bible books have been altered at some time in their history ('revisions').

To say that history has never had a 'definitive version' of the Bible is equally untrue. If the word 'version' refers to content, it must be admitted that the Roman Catholic church adds the Apocrypha (a collection of books between the Old and New Testaments), but no one suggests that anything should be added to the New Testament. The Old Testament and New Testament have been accepted by the church universally for two thousand years as final and definitive. However, if by 'version' he means that there are different translations, that is true, but in that case we do not have a definitive translation of the Gnostic writings either. Any reader can go online and choose which translator they wish to follow. All great works of literature are available in more than one translation.

CLAIM NO. 3

The claim is made that more than eighty gospels were considered for the New Testament: 'and yet only a relatively few were chosen for inclusion—Matthew, Mark, Luke and John among them.'

THE FACTS: There are a number of false 'gospels', but nothing like eighty! The total of *all* early documents written under assumed names that claim to be authentic 'scripture' (the technical word for this is *pseudepigrapha*) does not exceed sixty. Only a very few of these claim to be 'gospels' and five of those are in the Nag Hammadi Library; these 'gospels' are mostly fragments, not one recounts the story of the adult life of Christ, and all were clearly rejected by the early church. To say that only a relatively few were chosen, 'Matthew, Mark, Luke and John among them', implies that there were more. There never were any other gospels that were chosen by the early church—not one.

CLAIM NO. 4

Until the time of the Roman emperor Constantine in the fourth century, 'Jesus was viewed by his followers as a mortal prophet … a great and powerful man, but a *man*, nonetheless. A mortal.' However, at the Council of Nicea, called by Constantine in AD 325, the deity of Christ was put to the ballot and it scraped through by 'a relatively close vote.'

THE FACTS: The Council of Nicea did not invent the doctrine of the deity of Christ, it laid out a clear statement of what the great majority across the churches believed. Here is part of that creed:

We believe in one God the Father All-sovereign, maker of all things visible and invisible;

And in one Lord Jesus Christ, the Son of God, begotten of the Father, only-begotten, that is, of the substance of the Father, God of God, Light of Light, true God of true God, begotten not made, of one substance with the Father, through whom all things were made, things in heaven and things on earth; who for us men and for our salvation came down and was made flesh, and became man, suffered and rose on the third day, ascended into the heavens, is coming to judge the living and the dead.

Of course there were some who questioned the deity of Christ, and that was one reason why the Council was called. But the outcome was this clear statement that Christ is God and whilst distinct as a person, is essentially one with the Father. This is what the majority of churches across the Roman world clearly believed.

The claim that the deity of Christ was affirmed 'by a relatively close vote' is a strange way to describe a Council attended by nearly three hundred leaders of whom only two refused to sign what we know as the Nicean Creed.

CLAIM NO.5
'The Bible, as we know it today, was collated by the pagan Roman emperor Constantine the Great.' Constantine faced a problem because, 'thousands of documents already existed chronicling his [Jesus'] life as a mortal man', so the Emperor devised a bold action: 'the most profound moment in Christian history … The earlier gospels were outlawed, gathered up, and burned.'
THE FACTS: The idea that Constantine invented a new Bible is fantasy and has never been suggested by any historian, serious or otherwise. The four Gospels in the New Testament had been the only ones accepted for at least two hundred years before Constantine was born. However, what Dan Brown may have been mistakenly thinking about in his phrase 'Constantine commissioned and financed

a new Bible' is that in the year 332, the Emperor ordered his advisor and the first church historian, Eusebius of Caesarea, to arrange for fifty copies of the Scriptures to be prepared by skilled scribes and written carefully on the best parchment. There is not a shred of historical evidence that the Emperor was suggesting a rewriting of the text—he simply wanted to ensure that the whole Bible was carefully preserved.

Unfortunately Eusebius, usually very meticulous in this sort of thing, did not think to give us the list of books included in this Bible. However, we know from his writings elsewhere exactly what books were circulating as accepted by this time.

What does 'thousands of documents already existed chronicling his [Jesus'] life as a mortal man' mean? There were, perhaps, thousands of *copies* of these four Gospels circulating all over the Roman empire. But if it means thousands of different and conflicting documents, there is no evidence for this at all. Before AD 325, the four Gospels had been the only ones accepted for around two hundred years.

CLAIM NO.6
The novel asserts that the Dead Sea Scrolls and the Gnostic Scrolls 'highlight glaring historical discrepancies and fabrications' in the Bible. For this reason, the Vatican (the Roman Catholic hierarchy) tried to suppress the 'scrolls'. Thus 'almost everything our fathers taught us about Christ is false.' Teabing adds: 'Fortunately for historians, some of the gospels that Constantine attempted to eradicate managed to survive. The Dead Sea Scrolls were found in the 1950s hidden in a cave near Qumran in the Judean desert. And, of course, the Coptic Scrolls in 1945 at Nag Hammadi. In addition to telling the true Grail story, these documents speak of Christ's ministry in very human terms.'

THE FACTS: The idea that the Dead Sea Scrolls include some of the gospels that Constantine tried to destroy, or that they 'highlight glaring historical discrepancies and fabrications' in the Bible, or that they have anything to say about the Grail story or the life of Christ, is quite ridiculous. None of the Dead Sea Scrolls has anything to say about the Christian gospel since they are the records of a strict and monastic Jewish sect that had nothing to do with those outside their community. Most of the Dead Sea Scrolls were written long before Jesus died and they were discovered from 1947 and not 'in the 1950s'.

It is true that some academics have suggested that the beliefs of the community at the Dead Sea may have influenced the teaching of Jesus and the Christian church—a few even suggest that John the Baptist and Jesus were members of the community! However, it has been clearly shown that the contrasts between the teaching of the Qumran community and of the Christians are enormous: Members of the Dead Sea community were sworn to celibacy, had no desire to share their message with others and therefore would have had no contact with the Christians, they had no interest in the resurrection, did not believe in the Holy Spirit as a person or a present reality, had no concept of the Trinity, and taught their followers to 'hate their enemies'. In fact the only similarities are what they both share in common with the Old Testament.

As for the Nag Hammadi Library, these books could hardly make any comment on the historical details of the four Gospels since there is virtually no history in them at all; they are almost exclusively the supposed sayings of Jesus and his apostles. Many of their sayings contradict the plain teaching of the New Testament, but all the evidence is stacked against the Gnostic writings being any kind of reputable record of Jesus and his disciples.

As for the 'true Grail story', we have seen already exactly what the Gnostic records say about the marriage of Jesus and Mary.

If the Vatican had tried to suppress the publication of the Dead Sea Scrolls or the Nag Hammadi Library, this would have been such big news that we would not have needed Dan Brown's novel to inform us!

CLAIM NO.7

Brown claims that Constantine changed the Christian Sabbath from Saturday to Sunday.

THE FACTS: He certainly did not. It was the apostles who moved the day to Sunday which was the first day of the week (see Acts 20:7 and 1 Corinthians 16:2) and referred to it as 'the Lord's day' (Revelation 1:10). Dan Brown's confusion is that in AD 321, Constantine was the first to enact Sunday observance laws, but only because the day as special for Christians was already widespread.

CLAIM NO. 8

The novel refers to the legendary 'Q' Document that is a book of Jesus' teachings: 'possibly written by Jesus himself'. Admittedly this is a tentative suggestion—which is unusual in The Da Vinci Code—but it is certainly a novel idea.

THE FACTS: 'Q' is well known in academic circles as the hypothetical source of the sayings of Jesus that are common in some of the first three Gospels. No one has ever suggested that Jesus wrote it and we do not even know that it exists. But if it does, it makes no difference to anything that we have in the four Gospels.

CLAIM NO. 9

You may recall that we earlier quoted the claim of Teabing that 'The vast majority of educated Christians know the history of their faith.' This was in the context of the Nag Hammadi Library having effectively disproved the four Gospels.

THE FACTS: In reality the fact that educated Christians who know the history of their faith should be aware of is that, unlike the handful of long-lost Gnostic writings, we have literally thousands of Greek manuscripts of part or all of the four Gospels to help us to be sure that we have an accurate text. A number of these manuscripts are copies made in the second century and some scholars claim even to have discovered small portions that were copied in the first century.

This mass of evidence is far stronger than that of a small collection of abandoned books that had been lost for seventeen hundred years. How do we know that these fourth century copies of copies of the Gnostic writings are not full of copyists errors?

Dan Brown's knowledge of linguistics fails him, his grasp of church history is weak and his understanding of the transmission of the New Testament is sadly flawed.

8. When were the four Gospels accepted as Scripture?

In 1976 John A T Robinson, who was recognised as a first-class New Testament scholar though he did not believe in the total reliability of the Bible, published a book called *Redating the New Testament*. In this he concluded that the entire New Testament as we know it, had been completed before AD 70.

Robinson provided many very strong reasons for this, but one of the most convincing is the complete absence of any reference in the New Testament to the destruction of Jerusalem and the Temple in AD 70. In that year, the Roman army laid siege to the city and finally broke in, massacred its defenders and destroyed the Temple and the city. This is something that Jesus himself had prophesied, and we should expect that somewhere in their letters, at least one of the apostles would have used it as evidence of Jesus' authority and a symbol of the passing away of the Jewish faith now that the Messiah had come. But there is not even a hint in any New Testament book that Jerusalem and the Temple have been destroyed.

There can be only one of three reasons for this: either they did not know about it (ludicrously impossible), or there was a massive and well kept agreement, for reasons completely unknown to us, that they would not refer to it (hardly better as a suggestion), or it had not taken place at the time the Gospels and letters were written.

Robinson's conclusions are hard to deny, and they point to the circulation of the books of the New Testament long before the close of the first century.

But what do we learn from the church leaders themselves in the first two or three centuries? This is very important to show how far from the truth *The Da Vinci Code* really is.

THE CHURCH LEADERS HAD RULES ABOUT WHICH BOOKS WERE AUTHORITATIVE

Unlike the Gnostic writers, the early leaders never hesitated to contrast their own leadership with the authority of the apostles—and they never pretended to be apostles either.

Ignatius was the leader in the church at Antioch around the year AD 112, not long after the death of the apostle John. He contrasted himself with Peter and Paul saying, 'I do not, as Peter and Paul, issue commandments to you. They were apostles; I am but a condemned man.'

Polycarp was leader of the church at Smyrna and possibly the most influential church leader in Asia. He tells us that he was a Christian by the year AD 70 and had actually listened to the teaching of the apostles. Before his martyrdom in AD 156 he referred to himself in this way: 'For neither am I, nor is any other like me, able to follow the wisdom of the blessed and glorious Paul.'

In fact, the leaders of the churches severely punished anyone who wrote false letters (*pseudepigrapha*). In July AD 144, a wealthy Christian ship-owner from Pontus on the Black Sea was on trial for heresy before the leaders of the church in Rome. Among other things, this shipping magnate called Marcion accepted only Luke's Gospel and ten of Paul's letters—and even these he edited. Marcion was a Gnostic, and little wonder that he was excommunicated. But the fact that he could select books means that there were already accepted books in circulation.

Tertullian, well before AD 200, reports that a leader in an Asian church was severely disciplined when he admitted writing a document called the Acts of Paul—and he claimed that he had only done so because he admired Paul so much.

These church leaders also insisted that to be accepted as Scripture, books must be written by or with the influence of an apostle. How does this fit with the four Gospels—Matthew, Mark, Luke and John?

Matthew and John were both apostles, that is, among the Twelve specially selected disciples of Christ. But what of Mark and Luke? Two of the early church leaders, Papias and Tertullian, claimed that Mark wrote his Gospel in partnership with the apostle Peter. Papias was a leader in Phrygia early in the second century and he was very sure that:

> Mark, having become Peter's interpreter, wrote accurately all that he remembered without, however, recording in order the things said or done by the Lord ... So Mark committed no error as he wrote down some particulars just as he recalled them to mind. For he was careful of one thing—to omit nothing of what he had heard or to falsify anything in them.

Tertullian wrote against the Gnostic Marcion around AD 150 and he also insisted: 'That which Mark had published may be affirmed to be Peter's whose interpreter Mark was.' Similarly, Tertullian claimed: 'Even Luke's form of the Gospel, men usually ascribe to Paul.'

Another church leader, Irenaeus, writing around AD 180, agreed with this, as did Origen, writing from Alexandria in Egypt around AD 230.

HOW EARLY WERE THE FOUR GOSPELS BEING USED AMONG THE CHURCHES?

In 1740 an Italian scholar, Ludovico Muratori, published a document he had discovered in a library in Milan. It had been written originally some time before the middle of the second century AD (about the same time as Tertullian, mentioned above) and it contains the oldest known list of New Testament books. Not all the New Testament books are found in this list, but it includes the four Gospels—and no other gospels. This is known as the 'Muratorian Canon' (the word 'canon' means a rule or list).

Although as yet we do not have an official list of books earlier than this, it is quite clear that the leaders in the middle of the second century knew that the four Gospels belonged to the newly-formed New Testament.

There is plenty more evidence that long before the time of Constantine in the fourth century, the New Testament books—and no others—were accepted by the church as authoritative. Here is a summary, focusing only on the Gospels.

- Clement of Rome wrote a letter to Corinth about AD 95—and we could hardly expect anything much earlier than this. He quoted from Isaiah adding, 'and another Scripture however says, "I did not come to call the righteous but sinners."' This quotation comes from Matthew 9:13 and Clement called it 'Scripture'. So, as early as AD 95 the Gospel of Matthew was accepted as 'Scripture' by this church leader.

- Ignatius, the leader at Antioch and possibly the successor to the apostle Peter himself, was martyred in the year AD 112. From the amount of the New Testament that he quoted in his letters, some scholars believe that he must have known almost the whole of our New Testament—including the four Gospels.

- Papias and Tertullian (both mentioned above), by the middle of the second century, were familiar with all four Gospels.

- Around AD 150 Tatian wrote a harmony of the four Gospels, it is known as *Tatian's Diatessaron*. It is not easy to write a harmony of four books that have not yet been written!

- Justin Martyr, who died for his faith in AD 165, referred to all four Gospels.

- Irenaeus, writing around AD 180, was familiar with Mark and Luke, accepted them as written under the guidance of an apostle and, in an attack on the Gnostics, condemned those who deny that Jesus is God.

- Theophilus of Antioch in AD 180 was clearly acquainted with three of the four Gospels.

- Origen was a well-informed leader in Alexandria who, before his death in AD 253, knew what the churches everywhere believed. He reflected that belief when he wrote, 'The records of the Gospels [he was referring to the four] are oracles of the Lord, pure oracles as silver purified seven times in the fire …' Origen's New Testament contained all the twenty-seven books—and no more— when he wrote this.

- Early in the fourth century, Eusebius enquired into the attitude of all the churches and he listed what he called the recognised books, the disputed books and the rejected books. Under the first category Eusebius listed the four Gospels. Eusebius of Caesarea was an advisor to the Emperor Constantine and the first church historian. He was not making up a list, but discovering what the churches already accepted.

Therefore, long before the year AD 325, when Teabing thinks the four Gospels were imposed on the church, we have clear evidence that the four Gospels were accepted and in widespread circulation among the churches. Remember, there were a few other 'gospels' available in the first three hundred years, but they were firmly rejected as false by the church leaders right across the Roman empire and beyond. This is why the Gnostic books found at Nag Hammadi were discarded and lost for seventeen hundred years.

We can for ever reject the strange idea that for three hundred years after the death and resurrection of Christ there was an entirely different group of gospels circulating. The facts are that within twenty years of the death of the apostle John we have evidence of large parts of the New Testament being circulated and eagerly read by the young churches and, what is just as important, they were accepted as having an authority equal to that of the Old Testament. Throughout these early years of the church, leaders and teachers were quoting New Testament books as Scripture—and no other writings—to prove their doctrine.

Dan Brown's knowledge of the formation of the New Testament canon is not strong.

9. Where does da Vinci enter the story?

The novel begins in an art gallery in the Louvre Museum in Paris where a work of Leonardo da Vinci holds a vital secret that will be decoded later in the novel. However, it is his painting known as *The Last Supper* that is significant in the plot. Leonardo da Vinci was an Italian painter, sculptor, architect, musician, engineer and scientist who was born in 1452 and is known for his famous *Mona Lisa* painting. However, the theory of Teabing is that Leonardo da Vinci was one of the Grand Masters of the Priory of Sion, the society that held the secret of the Holy Grail. More than this, da Vinci coded a secret into one of his most well-known paintings, *The Last Supper,* which he painted on the wall of a convent in Milan in 1497.

Dan Brown's novel claims that the figure of a clean-shaven young man to the right of Jesus at the table is not, as has always been assumed, that of the apostle John, but is none other than Mary Magdalene herself. Looked at closely, the face is very much like that of a woman. Similarly, the gap between Jesus and 'Mary' reveals the V-shape symbolising the woman's womb, or the sacred feminine, and the figures of Jesus and 'Mary' outline the letter 'M'. In addition, there is no cup (or grail) on the table because da Vinci wants us to focus elsewhere for the Holy Grail. *That* is the Da Vinci Code.

Dan Brown maintains in his novel that 'All descriptions of artwork, architecture, documents and secret rituals in this novel are accurate'. That is a massively misleading claim. In response to this eccentric view of *The Last Supper* only a few points are needed.

- Not a single art historian has ever suggested that the figure to the right of Jesus was intended as any other than the apostle John.
- Da Vinci, along with many of the Renaissance painters, frequently portrayed young men in a rather effeminate way. Most of these artists represent John as young, fair and clean shaven. Some have seen this as evidence of da Vinci's homosexual tendencies, but this is conjecture. Robert Baldwin, Associate Professor of Art History at Connecticut College in the USA, has pointed out that after the year 1300 there was a revival of interest in the portrayal of young men by Renaissance artists, and he lists seven of them.
- If the figure is Mary Magdalene, then da Vinci has not accounted for all the apostles, for there are only thirteen figures at the table including Jesus—and Judas is clearly one of them, so it cannot be claimed that he had left.
- Da Vinci always worked on sketches of his paintings first, and in Venice there is the original sketch of *The Last Supper;* da Vinci has labelled this figure as John the apostle. Though, of course, that may be a scam!
- An early sixteenth-century copy of *The Last Supper* also labels this figure as 'Johannes'. Though, of course, that artist may not have been in on the plot!
- The absence of a cup is taken to indicate that this is early on in the meal, before the symbolic 'breaking of bread'.

However, even if we suppose that one day it is proved beyond doubt that da Vinci did intend his painting of the Last Supper to contain these hidden codes, what difference would that make to our knowledge and understanding of the four Gospels and the story of Christ? None whatsoever. Leonardo da Vinci in the fourteenth century would be entitled to his opinions, but his pictures are not our final or best commentary on early documents and the Bible.

10. Where did Dan Brown get his ideas from?

It is more than a little odd that the New York *Daily Times* included in its rave review of Dan Brown's novel: 'His research is impeccable'! We have already seen that Dan Brown's research into the origin of the New Testament and his knowledge of church history is not strong. But in reality, little of this is his own original thinking.

THE WORD

Even the theme of Dan Brown's book is not new. Back in 1972 Irving Wallace wrote a best-selling novel called *The Word,* in which two documents were discovered in ancient Roman foundations. One was supposedly the Gospel of James the brother of Jesus, and the other was a parchment of Petronius, one of Pilate's staff officers, who claimed that Jesus did not die on the cross but came round and lived a further nineteen years. Since this novel was written five years before the translation of the Nag Hammadi Library into English, this could not be included in the plot.

There *is* a Gospel of James. It was first discovered in 1958 and is dated around the third century; it is not part of the Nag Hammadi Library. It deals with little more than the birth of Mary the mother of Jesus, her story up to the birth of Christ, and a little of the early life of Jesus. Clearly the writer, whoever he was, had access to Matthew and Luke, but for good reasons this document was never taken seriously by the early church.

Unfortunately the unwary reader of *The Word* may forget that the entire centrepiece of the novel is pure fiction, because, like *The Da Vinci Code,* so much 'certainty' is woven in. For example, a reference to the Gospels asserts: 'These four Gospel writers had not lived with Jesus, observed him, seen him in the flesh. They had merely collected oral traditions, some writings from the early Christian community, and transcribed them onto papyrus decades after the supposed death of Jesus. All this was frozen into the immutable canon that became our New Testament in the third or fourth century ... The modern biblical experts know that the present four gospels are not factual history ... [They] are largely a series of myths strung together.'

This is an extremely old fashioned view of the four Gospels, but it is easy to see where Dan Brown got his ideas from for the basic plot of his novel.

Part of the story line of *The Word* reveals how easily a gullible world can be taken in by a good forgery. However, perhaps significantly, *The Word* closes with the murder of the one man who could have verified whether or not the parchment of Petronius was a forgery. Perhaps we are expected to assume that if the world in the novel could be conned by such a forgery, in real life we are all equally likely to have swallowed a lie with the four Gospels.

THE HOLY BLOOD AND THE HOLY GRAIL

Of more significant value to Dan Brown, for without it his novel would never have been written, is *The Holy Blood and the Holy Grail* by three authors, Baigent, Leigh and Lincoln. Published first in 1982, it too was a best-seller, but was not strictly a novel. It was a serious investigation into the identity of the Holy Grail. The research began with the parish priest in the French village of Rennes-le-Chateau, delved into the Crusades and the Knights Templars, the Merovingian line of French royalty, and the secret order of the Priory of Sion of which, among others, Robert Boyle, Isaac Newton and Leonardo de Vinci were Grand Masters.

Whilst the authors began with serious research—though with scores of assumptions and hypotheses to build the case—the book descends into wild accusations against the trustworthiness of the four Gospels: 'The more one studies the Gospels, the more the contradictions between them become apparent', and even more extreme speculations: 'The Gnostic Gospels enjoyed as great a claim to veracity as the books of the New Testament'. The final hypothesis provides Dan Brown with his cue: 'a bloodline descended from Jesus which has continued up to the present day'. This, the authors insist, is 'essentially accurate.' Along the way, among the many bizarre suggestions are that Christ did not die on the cross and even Barabbas might have been his son!

Unlike Dan Brown, these authors do not commit themselves to a single child (Jesus could have had many), but they, like Brown, are waiting for the Priory of Sion to come forward with its conclusive evidence. Dan Brown acknowledges his use of this book, but in fact all his research material is found here and he has added virtually nothing in his novel to the research of *The Holy Blood and the Holy Grail*. Even the play with *San Greal* and *Sang Réal* is found here first.

11. What is Dan Brown's real agenda?

There is no doubt that Dan Brown had his own agenda for writing the book other than to create a popular novel. He claims to be a Christian, after a sort, and refutes any idea that the book is anti-Christian, claiming: 'This book is not anti-anything.' Brown set out to explore 'certain aspects of Christian history that interest me.' Whilst he offers his work as a good point for discussion and humbly claims only that, 'it is my belief that some of the theories discussed by these characters may have merit', this is, as we said at the beginning, a little devious because of the way the book is cast. Statements are made that the average reader has no way of easily checking and they are not offered as interpretations or discussion points, but 'facts' of history. There are three agendas that clearly show through.

PROMOTING THE SACRED FEMININE

Dan Brown admits to an agenda to promote the sacred feminine. The whole thrust is that the New Testament was written by the winners in the struggle for supremacy, and those winners were the men: 'Powerful men in the early Christian church "conned" the world by propagating lies that devalued the female and tipped the scales in favour of the masculine.' From the fourth century on, it was men alone who occupied the centre stage on the Christian scene, and it is now time that history was rewritten to reflect the leadership of women up to that point.

In response, we have already seen that the New Testament books were completed and circulating well before the close of the first century, but we can add that there are no ancient documents that speak so highly of women and guard their value with such care as the New Testament does. The Gospels are unashamed in their record of the faithful ministry (Luke 8:1–3 and Mark 15:40–41), deep spiritual devotion (Mark 14:1–6), and outstanding courage of the women (John 19:25). They were the first to see Jesus alive after the resurrection and the first to announce his resurrection to the apostles. In the letters of Paul and Peter women are to be loved by their husbands 'as Christ loved the church' (Ephesians 5:25) and are to be treated with 'consideration' and 'respect' (1 Peter 3:7).

But there is more to the novel than this. We are to suppose that as in ancient religion, so even in Judaism and early Christianity there was a belief in the female deity—a goddess: 'Early Jews believed that the Holy of Holies in Solomon's Temple housed not only God, but also his powerful female equal, Shekinah.' The novel makes great play on the 'sacred feminine'. The church from Constantine to the present day has 'demonized the sacred feminine, obliterating the goddess from modern religion for ever.' This belief in a goddess must be restored.

PRESENTING SEX AS A SACRAMENT

It had to come in somewhere. The only point at which sex enters the novel is when Sophie retells the disgusting sex rituals of the Priory of Sion, and at this point the story takes the inevitable titillating twist that doubtless the movie will exploit to the full. Sex becomes a sacrament in which God is experienced. We are taken back to the ancient goddess Isis, and the sexual experience is that which leads as a pathway to God. We are assured that this was an experience of God which the Jews and early Christians were all involved in. We have noted already the claim that the Shekinah in the Temple of Solomon was known to be a powerful female equal to God. Even the divine name, Yahweh, is turned into a sex symbol.

All this is a blasphemous slander that is wholly without a shred of historical or linguistic evidence and is clearly contradicted by the New Testament teaching on the purity of marriage as the only context for sexual union.

The evidence of early documents is that the Gnostics were condemned by the church leaders for, on the one hand, dismissing all material things as evil, and yet on the other, enjoying some particularly sordid pleasures. Jude, writing in the New Testament, had this kind of thing in his sights when he wrote about 'Godless men, who change the grace of our God into a licence for immorality and deny Jesus Christ our only Sovereign and Lord', and he compared them to the men of Sodom and Gomorrah who 'gave themselves up to sexual immorality and perversion' (Jude 4,7).

That is clearly how the New Testament writers would have dismissed *The Da Vinci Code*.

DENYING THAT JESUS IS GOD

Perhaps the most serious challenge of *The Da Vinci Code* is that it denies the claim that Jesus was truly God. There is no doubt that this denial is fundamental to the novel. This, apparently, was a main reason for the 'new Bible' to be written in the fourth century; before this, he 'was viewed by his followers as a mortal prophet ... a great and powerful man, but a *man*, nonetheless. A mortal.'

However, to suggest that the four Gospels simply invented a story of Jesus to show that he was divine and not mortal—omitting those gospels 'that spoke of Christ's *human* traits'—reveals how little the author has read his New Testament.

In reality the Gospels reveal the humanness of Jesus on many occasions: he had a human mother and grew up as a child, he worked, became tired and slept, could be hungry and thirsty and he ate and drank, he could be angry and compassionate, he was tempted as we are, and needed to pray. None of this would have been written if the church was out to make him God and nothing more.

The entire New Testament maintains the balance of the deity and humanity of Jesus.

It is a fact that the letters of Paul in the New Testament were circulating at the same time, some would say even before, the Gospels. Paul wrote his letters between the years AD 48 and 64, and he was adamant that Jesus is God. Here are a few examples of the claim in Paul's New Testament letters for the fact that Christ is God:

'Who [Jesus], being in very nature God ... made himself nothing, taking the very nature of a servant' (Philippians 2:6–7).

'In Christ all the fulness of the Deity lives in bodily form' (Colossians 2:9).

'About the Son he says, "Your throne, O God, will last for ever and ever"' (Hebrews 1:8).

'We wait for the blessed hope—the glorious appearing of our great God and Saviour, Jesus Christ' (Titus 2:13).

Certainly there is no doubt that this is exactly how the Jews understood him:

'"We are ... stoning you for ... blasphemy, because you, a mere man, claim to be God"' (John 10:33).

'The Jews tried all the harder to kill him, not only was he breaking the

Sabbath, but he was even calling God his own Father, making himself equal with God' (John 5:18).

'"I tell you the truth," Jesus answered, "before Abraham was born, I am!" At this, they picked up stones to stone him' (John 8:58).

'The Pharisees and the teachers of the law began thinking to themselves, "Who is this fellow who speaks blasphemy? Who can forgive sins but God alone?"' (Luke 5:21).

This is all very different from Dan Brown's assertion that until the year 325 no one thought of Christ as God.

12. In summary
- There is no evidence at all that Jesus married Mary Magdalene—or anyone.
- There is no evidence at all that in the time of Constantine a new gospel was invented, written and forced on the churches.
- There is plenty of evidence that the four Gospels were circulating more than two hundred years before Constantine became Emperor—and they alone were accepted by the churches.
- There is plenty of evidence that from the earliest time the churches believed that Jesus was both truly Man and truly God.
- Even if the mysterious and covert Priory of Sion holds the secret story of a supposed blood-line of Jesus, it would *prove* nothing. It would be no more than another legend invented by those who cannot resist the temptation either to add to the record of the Bible or to undermine the truthfulness of its message.

Finally—What is the truth?
What happened to the Gnostics? They simply died out and their documents were lost, apart from a couple of texts discovered in the nineteenth century and the more recent Nag Hammadi Library. No one should be taken in or shaken by the 'revelations' of *The Da Vinci Code*, because the book has no claim to scholarship or history, and even less claim to honesty.

On the other hand, the New Testament has been on trial and tested for almost two thousand years. It has been banned, burned, and subjected to the most stringent critical analysis.

No piece of literature has had more books written about it than the Bible. But it stands unscathed.

The Bible has been called an anvil that has worn out many hammers.

The Da Vinci Code is yet another hammer.

What, then, is the essential message of the New Testament?

The good news is about Jesus as the Messiah, promised by the prophets and expected by the Jews. He was the Son of God, co-equal with the Father, and perfect in every way. His mission was to reveal:

* the heart of God for the world by his care and compassion
* the power of God over the universe by his miracles
* the righteous anger of God against sin by his suffering on the cross
* the love of God for sinners by his willing death in their place
* and the assured promises of God by his resurrection and ascension

To all this, the four Gospels and the letters of the apostles—all completed and circulating by the end of the first century—agree without a single exception or contradiction.

Jesus once claimed:

'I am the way and the truth and the life. No one comes to the Father except through me ... Anyone who has seen me has seen the Father' (John 14:6,9).

The Da Vinci Code will have served at least some useful purpose, if those who read it are persuaded by its ill-conceived and dishonest claims that the truth is far better, and that, by contrast, Jesus Christ is worthy of our love, obedience and adoration.

Some books for further reading

Nothing But The Truth by Brian H Edwards. pub. Evangelical Press new edition 2006.

Covers the whole subject of the reliability and history of our Bible and written in an accessible way for those without prior knowledge of the subject.

The Canon of the New Testament by Bruce M Metzger. pub. Clarenden Press 1987.

How and when the books of the New Testament were accepted by the church is a detailed subject. This book will require some determined reading, but is an excellent discussion of the issues involved.

The Dead Sea Scrolls and the Originality of Christ by Geoffrey Graystone. pub. Sheed and Ward 1956.

There are many books on the Dead Sea Scrolls, but this is for those who are troubled by the suggestion that there may be a relationship between the early church and the Qumran community that is hinted at in *The Da Vinci Code*. This book contrasts the beliefs of the Qumran community with those of Jesus and the early Christians.

Breaking the Da Vinci Code by Darrell L Brock. pub. Thomas Nelson Inc. 2004.

Of the many books responding to Dan Brown's novel, this is one of the best. Written by a highly qualified author, it is not hard to follow.

The Da Vinci Code on Trial by Stephen Clark. pub. Bryntirion Press 2005.

A careful sifting of the evidence against Dan Brown's claims and looking at the real evidence for Jesus.

TRACTS ON THE SUBJECT

The Da Vinci Code—a response by Nicky Gumbel. pub. Alpha International 2005.

A small format, thirty page booklet covering the most important points in the debate. Recommended.

Vinci De Coded by Roger Carswell. pub. Key to Life Tracts 2005.

A very brief tract but excellent as a giveaway.

© Day One Publications 2006 First printed 2006

All Scripture quotations are taken from the New International Version

A CIP record is held at The British Library   ISBN 1 84625 019 6

Published by Day One Publications Ryelands Road, Leominster, England, HR6 8NZ

☎ 01568 613 740 FAX 01568 611 473 email—sales@dayone.co.uk www.dayone.co.uk

Design: Steve Devane   Printed by Gutenberg Press, Malta